LENT

A Journey of Discovery
by Addition, Subtraction and Introspection

Erik E. Willits

LENT: A Journey of Discovery
by Addition, Subtraction and Introspection

Copyright © 2013 by Erik E. Willits

Publisher: Mark Oestreicher
Managing Editor: Anne Jackson
Cover Design: Adam McLane
Layout: Marilee R. Pankratz
Creative Director: God

ISBN-10: 0-9887413-1-8
ISBN-13: 978-0-9887413-1-7

The Youth Cartel, LLC
www.theyouthcartel.com
Email: info@theyouthcartel.com
Born in San Diego
Printed in the U.S.A.

Table of Contents

Welcome to a Journey of Discovery

Lent is the time in the Christian year that leads us to Easter and our celebration of the resurrection of Jesus. For most of my Christian life, I was aware of Lent but didn't engage in the creative aspects Christians have participated in for hundreds of years. However, for the past several years, my engagement in Lenten exercises has provided water for my thirsty soul. Lent is usually a period marked by prayer, penitential activities, helping those in need and radical self-denial.

I have simplified those ideas in my own life focusing on three things. With the hope and expectation of participating in the resurrection, during Lent I will:

- add something,
- subtract something, and
- spend intentional time in self examination.

My hope is that this book would also guide you and whoever wants to join you in a journey of discovery by addition, subtraction and introspection.

The idea for this guide to Lent is that you will enter into this journey with your church, youth group, small group or family. This adventure of following Jesus through the desert to the cross and ultimately participating with Him in the resurrection is not to be done alone. I hope that this book you hold in your hand helps you and your community along the way.

Let's begin this amazing and deep journey through the desert to the cross, and ultimately be prepared to participate in the resurrection!

Erik Willits

How to Use This Book...

A 40-day journey? That's a pretty long trek. If you've never heard of Lent before, you may be wondering what you're getting yourself into, or how this book will serve to guide you along the way. It's actually pretty simple. Here's how it works.

This book is comprised of scripture readings, reflections and questions for every day of the journey. Each day you'll engage the different readings with your family, your friends or maybe on your own. Our journey begins with Ash Wednesday and ends with Easter, so think of those events as bookends. The 40 days in between are grouped into seven Lenten themes: Dust, Desert, Tempt, Aware, Desire, Crossed, and Approach. Each week you'll study and explore the given theme, drawing you deeper into the experience.

Every day of the week will start off with a Bible reading. This scripture has been intentionally left out of this book so that you can engage with the passage in your own Bible. Highlight the passage, take notes, doodle...use the physical pages in your Bible as part of the journey. It may be easy to skip over this part and head straight into the meditation. I encourage you to take the extra minute or two, sit down with your Bible and read the Scripture for the day. If you only do one thing, do this. After the Scripture, you'll find a brief devotional thought and then a meditation from a writer, scholar, thinker or interesting person. These meditations will help you think more deeply about that week's theme. They can be challenging—including some big theological words and maybe ideas you haven't thought about before—but don't be discouraged. If you don't understand something, ask someone in your community or a parent, and you can even email me (my information is included in the back of the book). I would love to listen to your questions and help you find answers.

On Sundays, you will find four Scripture readings from the Lectionary, a book of scripture readings churches all over the world use for their worship services. Reading the same Scriptures as thousands of other Christians around the world helps us remember that we are a part of something amazing and big. We are not alone on this Lenten journey.

We will also engage in three disciplines Christians have commonly practiced during Lent. I've phrased them like this: addition, subtraction and introspection. These practices are not mandatory, but they will help us to make the most of this Lenten journey, deepen our experience and go places spiritually that maybe we've never been before. Let me explain.

3

Addition

Often during Lent, Christians take on or add extra spiritual practices. It could be praying for an extra five minutes every morning when you wake up. It could be extra Bible reading or journaling every night before you fall asleep. It could be doing a daily act of kindness for someone or giving extra money to people in need around the world. Whatever it is, during Lent this "addition" to your life will help you open your heart and mind to the work Christ wants to do in your life.

Subtraction

You may have heard people talk about what they're "giving up" for Lent. I encourage you to "subtract" something from your life that you depend on or enjoy on a daily basis. Subtract listening to the radio, eating candy or playing video games. People often give up meat or caffeine. Giving up that Starbucks might be challenging, but it could be just what you need to do. Subtract checking Facebook, Twitter or one of your other daily internet habits. Giving up these things makes more time for God and every time you crave that thing, let prayer and dependence upon God fill that space in your life.

Introspection

Introspection means exploring your inner thoughts and feelings, taking time to stop and search your heart before God. We're often too busy to pause to think about our true motivations and reactions, especially when it means awareness of our own pain and sinfulness. In the Psalms, David asks God to search him and know him; during these 40 days that is exactly what we hope is happening. We invite God to search us and know us, reveal to us all the wickedness that hides in the shadows of our heart. Think deeply about where you are in life and in relation to God. He will help you. It might be uncomfortable, but you'll learn things about yourself that you didn't know before.

Again, if you are confused or struggling with anything during this Lenten journey, don't hesitate to get help. You're not in this alone.

Now, let's get started on the unforgettable road to resurrection!

The Lent Web Guide is a supplement to this book. There, you will find images and icons, videos, more great meditative quotes and Bible reading, as well as an opportunity to leave comments, ask questions and share a bit of your journey through this time of Lent.

www.LentWebGuide.com

As you're reading, look for these icons.

SNAP!
There's a picture, image or Christian icon for you to check out!

You're only a click away.
We've posted a link to a website, blog or something cool for you to look at!

We've got a great video, YouTube, Vimeo or other goodie for you to watch.

Listen up!
We've posted an audio clip, sermon or message for you to listen to!

We like the Bible around here!
When you see this, we've got more Scripture for you!

Get ready to be inspired!
We've posted a quote or meditation that you won't want to miss.

There's an app for that.
We've provided a link to an app for your smart phone that might help you on this journey.

It's time to experiment!
Get ready to experiment with living out what you're learning!

Factoring In Failure

Maybe you're not like me. Maybe you are extremely self-disciplined and whenever you set your mind to do something, you do it flawlessly! Awesome! You probably have some other things you need to work out with the Lord, but definitely not the same things I do. You see, me—I'm a failure! I regularly fail at things I say I'm going to do...waking up in the morning to pray, reading my Bible every day, not doing this or that...FAIL, FAIL and #FAIL once again! (hashtag for public emphasis—Twitter peeps will understand!)

Lent is a time of self-denial, of extra spiritual focus and discipline... but if you do it all perfectly and fail to be engaged in your humanity and this journey toward the cross, well, you have failed! It's not about failing on purpose, but it's about realizing that if you do mess up, slip up or eat up one day because you just didn't think about it, or because you just had to see that show, or because you couldn't go one more moment without a smoke or a drink (coffee or otherwise)...It's Lent! Maybe in your failure, you can "get it" even more, in an even deeper kind of way.

So, I don't plan for failure; I don't put an X on my Lent calendar to mark the day I will fail, but I pretty much factor in the fact that I will fail—there will be a day I utterly fall on my face, whether it is with my Lenten discipline or in some other area of my life. And in that moment, I stop, pray and remember that I am nothing but dust! I know that I journey in the desert of temptation with the only person who has ever done it perfectly. Jesus is my only hope! I continue to follow Him through the desert to the cross and ultimately participate with Him in the resurrection!

Factor in some failure this Lent! Be ready for it so that when it happens, you're ready to pray, think and continue on!

"The goal of Lent is not to make a plan for change and follow it to the letter. Rather, the goal is to make a change that sinks deeply into life, drawing us closer to self, others, and God. Lent is about intentionally opening ourselves, preparing to receive God's goodness."

— From *A Clearing Season: Reflections for Lent* by Sarah Parsons

DUST

DUST // DAY 1 ASH WEDNESDAY
READING :: Genesis 2:4-7

It's hard to say that you're looking forward to Lent. That's like saying you like pain or punishment. But even though Lenten discipline can be very difficult, I always look forward to this time of year. I anticipate adding things of spiritual value to my life and subtracting or purging my life of unnecessary things. More than anything, I need this time that the church dedicates to looking inward, corporately and individually, walking through the desert en route to the cross and ultimately to resurrection.

Ash Wednesday invites us into the Lenten season by marking our foreheads with a cross made of ash by which we are told either to "Remember that we are dust..." or to "Repent and believe the Gospel." This day turns our attention to Jesus' cross and to the way we live our lives.

Christians often observe Ash Wednesday by attending a special church service. I lived in Nashville, Tennessee, and just about every year, I attended Ash Wednesday services at Christ Church Cathedral, a large, beautiful Episcopal church in the heart of the city. When you walk into a place like this, it may seem old and dingy, but every crack is filled with history and beauty—from the stained glass that helps you see the truth of God's kingdom, to the grandiose pillars and carved wood, to the echoes of voices you're sure are hundreds of years old but are actually coming from the choir loft. I loved being invited to kneel and receive ashes, read the 51st Psalm and confess my sins. It always seemed like the perfect way to begin the Lenten journey.

As you begin your own Lenten journey this Ash Wednesday, allow yourself to wonder about these 40 days of reflection, prayer and fasting, seeking Jesus and journeying with Him and each other. What will they hold for you? How will they change you? I pray the following liturgy will help you more fully experience the meaning of Ash Wednesday and enter into Lent.

Ash Wednesday Liturgy
Adapted from the 1979 Book of Common Prayer

Prayer :: Almighty and everlasting God, you hate nothing you have made and forgive the sins of all who are penitent: Create and make in us new and contrite hearts, that we, worthily lamenting our sins and acknowledging our wretchedness, may obtain of you, the God of all mercy, perfect remission and forgiveness; through Jesus Christ our Lord, who lives and reigns with you and the Holy Spirit, one God, for ever and ever. Amen.

READINGS
Isaiah 58:1-12 :: Psalm 103 ::
2 Corinthians 5:20-6:10 :: Matthew 6:1-6, 16-21

Almighty God, you have created us out of the dust of the earth: Grant that these ashes may be to us a sign of our mortality and penitence, that we may remember that it is only by your gracious gift that we are given everlasting life; through Jesus Christ our Savior. Amen.

Remember that you are dust, and to dust you shall return. *(These words are spoken when ashes are put on your forehead. Even if you don't hear it, you should be thinking about it today.)*

LITANY OF PENITENCE

This entire liturgy is best done in community. Have a leader read and all other participants respond with the phrases in bold. Best done on your knees.

Most holy and merciful Father: We confess to you and to one another, and to the whole communion of saints in heaven and on earth, that we have sinned by our own fault in thought, word, and deed; by what we have done, and by what we have left undone.

We have not loved you with our whole heart, and mind, and strength. We have not loved our neighbors as ourselves. We have not forgiven others, as we have been forgiven.
[Have mercy on us, Lord.]

9

We have been deaf to your call to serve, as Christ served us. We have not been true to the mind of Christ. We have grieved your Holy Spirit.
[Have mercy on us, Lord.]

SIN AGAINST SELF

We confess to you, Lord, all our past unfaithfulness: the pride, hypocrisy, and impatience of our lives,
[We confess to you, Lord.]

Our self-indulgent appetites and ways, and our exploitation of other people,
[We confess to you, Lord.]

Our anger at our own frustration, and our envy of those more fortunate than ourselves,
[We confess to you, Lord.]

Our intemperate love of worldly goods and comforts, and our dishonesty in daily life and work,
[We confess to you, Lord.]

Our negligence in prayer and worship, and our failure to commend the faith that is in us,
[We confess to you, Lord.]

SINS AGAINST OUR NEIGHBOR

Accept our repentance, Lord, for the wrongs we have done: for our blindness to human need and suffering, and our indifference to injustice and cruelty,
[Accept our repentance, Lord.]

For all false judgments, for uncharitable thoughts toward our neighbors, and for our prejudice and contempt toward those who differ from us,
[Accept our repentance, Lord.]

SINS AGAINST CREATION

For our waste and pollution of your creation, and our lack of concern for those who come after us,
[Accept our repentance, Lord.]

Restore us, good Lord, and let your anger depart from us,
[Favorably hear us, for your mercy is great.]

Accomplish in us the work of your salvation,
[That we may show forth your glory in the world.]

By the cross and passion of your Son our Lord,
[Bring us with all your saints to the joy of his resurrection.]

After the Litany of Penitence, it might be helpful to spend some time in prayer and meditation on some of the Scripture readings.
Try focusing on Psalm 103 during this time.

I once heard someone say, "I need Ash Wednesday because I live like I'm never going to die."

I think that we need Ash Wednesday and Lent because we too live like we are never going to die.

Today, like yesterday, let us stop and remember that from dust we came and to dust we will return -- that our life is a gift and we would be nothing more than dust if it were not for God. We should remember this every Sabbath: that the world doesn't revolve around our efforts or what we have, including our very lives. Everything is a gift from God. We deepen that lesson again today and during the season of Lent.

Here is a Franciscan Blessing to reflect on today.

May God bless you with discomfort. Discomfort at easy answers, half truths and superficial relationships, so that you may live deep within your heart. Amen

May God bless you with anger. Anger at injustice, oppression and exploitation of people, so that you may work for justice, freedom and peace. Amen

May God bless you with tears. Tears to shed for those who suffer from pain, rejection, starvation and war, so that you may reach out your hand to comfort them and turn their pain into joy. Amen

May God bless you with foolishness. Enough foolishness to believe that you can make a difference in this world, so that you can do what others claim cannot be done. Amen

And the blessing of God, who creates, redeems and sanctifies, be upon you and all you love and pray for this day, and forever more. Amen

Have you thought about your life as a gift lately?

In today's culture, we don't like to think about our own mortality. In fact, we try to act like death doesn't exist. It often makes us feel sad, fearful, uncomfortable or depressed. But during Lent, rather than denying the reality of death and the brevity of our own lives, we ponder these things. We pause to accept our own fragile state of humanity. We learn not to take our lives for granted. Today's meditation reminds us to shoulder the responsibility to live the kinds of lives that count, no matter how long they last.

MEDITATION ::.

Very quickly there will be an end of you here; look what will become of you in another world. Today the man is here, tomorrow he has disappeared. And when he is out of sight, quickly also is he out of mind.

Oh, the stupidity and hardness of man's heart, which thinks only upon the present and does not rather care for what is to come.

You ought to order yourself in all your thoughts and actions, as if today you will die.

If today you are not prepared, how will you be tomorrow? Tomorrow is uncertain, and how do you know that you will live till tomorrow?

When it is morning think that you might die before night.

And when evening comes, dare not to promise yourself the next morning.

Therefore you should always be ready, and so lead a life that death may never take you unprepared.

Labor now to live so, that at the hour of death you may rather rejoice than fear.

Learn now to die to the world, so that you may then begin to live with Christ. Learn now to despise all earthly things, that you may freely live with Christ. Ah, foolish me, why do you think to live long, when you can not promise to you one day.

—from *The Imitation of Christ* by Thomas a Kempis.

What are your thoughts about death?
Are you living carelessly like this world is all there is?

In today's reading, the Psalmist frankly shares with God his thoughts on life and death. He seems well aware of his own mortality and takes the opportunity to remind God that all of humankind's days on earth are few. Meanwhile, he pours out his frustrations about the seeming pointlessness of life and the inevitable fate that awaits us all.

It's during Lent that prayers and Psalms like this one lead us into honest and vulnerable places of prayer and reflection. Let today's Psalm remind you of the kind of prayers God's people pray, and let this Lenten journey be a time for you to join in.

Psalm 89:46-51 ::.
How long, LORD? Will you hide yourself forever?
How long will your wrath burn like fire?
Remember how fleeting is my life.
For what futility you have created all humanity!
Who can live and not see death,
or who can escape the power of the grave?
Lord, where is your former great love,
which in your faithfulness you swore to David?
Remember, Lord, how your servant has been mocked,
how I bear in my heart the taunts of all the nations,
the taunts with which your enemies, LORD, have mocked, with which they have mocked every step of your anointed one.

Have you ever considered how few days your life takes up
in the course of human history?
What does this thought stir in your heart and soul?

LENT :: Sunday #1
Genesis 9:8-17 | 1 Peter 3:18-22
Psalm 25:1-9 | Mark 1:9-15

Our Sunday readings are from the Revised Common Lectionary, year B. If your community follows the lectionary make sure you check which lectionary year is being followed. The resource on the Lent Web Guide can help you with this. My hope is that you read these verses, meditate on them and engage them on Sunday morning with your church community. If your church doesn't follow the Lectionary, it's still powerful to know that thousands of Christians around the world are reading and thinking about these same verses. You're a part of something big: You're not on this Lenten journey alone!

I use a few key resources to help me connect to the Lectionary, Bible reading and the church calendar during this season. Check out the Lent Web Guide to get your hands on these resources.

DESERT

DESERT // DAY 6
READING :: Matthew 4:1-11

Did you know that Lent parallels the 40 days Jesus spent in the wilderness without food and while being tempted by the devil? For us, Lent is 40 days we spend in a metaphorical wilderness, or a desert as the Bible often explains it, with dry mouths, empty bellies and open hearts. A common Lenten practice is to deprive ourselves of some of our favorite and seemingly most important things for spiritual benefit. This might be a favorite food, caffeine, video games, or, if you're hard core, the Internet (it's hard—I tried it one year). Many people also add something to their lives during Lent: a daily Bible reading or devotional, a regular act of service, or giving an extra 10% of their income or allowance to the Lord's work.

Whatever it is that you subtract or add to your life, the point is that we spend these days in the desert, taking on extra prayer and meditation, giving up luxuries and distractions with Jesus right beside us. We remember that He too spent 40 days in the desert, fasting, praying, meditating and being tempted. We don't do this perfectly: In fact, we are like the generations and generations of people who have fallen and failed, who have succumbed to the hunger, the thirst, the temptation that the desert brings. Jesus is the only one who did not fail. That's important to remember as we journey for 40 days with Jesus in the desert of self-denial, temptation and self-examination.

Maybe you heard a sermon at church yesterday on Matthew 4:1-11 or a similar passage. (This verse was also one of our readings yesterday.) If you were able to listen to a sermon, I hope it centers you in this week of reflection on desert and temptation. If you weren't able to listen to a related message, check out the Lent Web Guide for some recommended listening.

What temptations have you encountered
as you've been thinking and fasting?

Yesterday, we discussed the parallels between Jesus' 40-day journey in the desert and our 40 days of Lent. Today we think about similar parallels between Jesus' 40 days in the desert, and the 40 years the Hebrews spent wandering in the desert wilderness on their way to the Promised Land. The Hebrew people came through the water of the Red Sea, led by God, affirmed by God's mighty deeds, and stumbled into the desert. Jesus came through the water of baptism, affirmed by the Father, and was thrust into the desert as well.

It's interesting to think about what Jesus did during His 40 days. We know He fasted, which was intimately connected to prayer and meditation. My guess is that as he experienced hunger and thirst, He struggled with the thoughts of what was ahead of Him. Did Jesus pray in those moments, "If there is another way, please do that ... But not my will but yours be done"?

Is this where He formulated the Lord's prayer? Were Jesus' 40 days of fasting, self denial, prayer and meditation hard for Him? I think they probably were. And we already know His 40 days finished with some good old-fashioned temptation— more than the temptation that He had already experienced to eat, to get out of the desert and go to a friend's house, to just get comfortable. But Jesus was faithful, all the way to the end.

Our story is more like the story of the Hebrews in Exodus, a story of wandering, temptation and lots of failure. Their story is our story. But Jesus' story is one of faithfulness. May the same Spirit who thrust Jesus into the desert wilderness be with you when you find yourself in the dry, desolate places of life during Lent, where temptation will inevitably come. It is that Spirit who is faithful and our flesh that is weak.

How does your time in the desert of Lent compare or contrast
to the time Jesus spent in the desert?

Do we ever just sit in our desert? In our dark night of the soul? In our dryness and spiritual barrenness? Do we ever simply sit and ponder the reality that we are nothing but dust and that our life is but a vapor? I propose that we don't think about these things very often. Why not? Too depressing maybe. As we talked about in Day 3, many of us think or at least live like we will never die. I heard a professor once say, "We are all dirt bags," referencing the Genesis account of God creating us out of the dirt. It's true, right? Maybe from time to time, especially in a season like Lent, it's humbling but helpful to sit there, to meditate on our humanity and mortality, to ponder our bent to wander and fail every step of the way.

Saint Francis de Sales in his book, *An Introduction to the Devout Life*, offers us some guiding meditation on this very subject:

> Humble yourself profoundly before God, acknowledging your nothingness and misery. Alas, what am I when left to myself? No better, Lord, than the parched ground, whose cracks and crevices on every side testify to its need of the gracious rain of Heaven, while, nevertheless, the world's blasts wither in more and more dust.

He goes on to give some specific meditation and guidance for those wandering in the desert. He says, "After all, nothing is so useful, so fruitful amid this dryness and barrenness, as not to yield to a passionate desire of being delivered from it." Saint Francis guides us to sit in our desert and reflect on where we are, letting this desert be a refining and preparatory place in our spiritual journey.

This week we observe and meditate on our location during Lent—the desert. How quickly do you usually ask to be delivered from the desert?

What stops you from sitting in the difficulty of life,
praying that God might show you what He wants to teach you?

DESERT // DAY 9
READING :: Hebrews 3:7-19

It's interesting to me how verse 8 of Hebrews Chapter 3 states, "Today, if you hear his voice, do not harden your hearts as you did in the rebellion during the time of testing in the wilderness, where your ancestors tested and tried me though for forty days they saw what I did."

This verse starts off with "... do not harden your hearts as you did" but quickly moves into "... where your ancestors tested and tried me..."

It seems that the author of Hebrews understands the fact that their story is our story. That we are prone to wander in the wilderness and we are bent to unbelief and faithlessness as humanity has always been.

Today's passage gives us a glimpse into the faithfulness of God but firmly reminds us of our tendency to wandering faithlessness. This juxtaposition is exactly what I want us to meditate on this week as we focus on the desert and what we would be if it were not for Jesus.

How have you hardened your heart against the Lord?

Just as the Israelites physically found themselves in the desert, so we can emotionally and spiritually find ourselves there. Today's meditation describes a place that may sound familiar to you—we have all spent time in that hard, dry land at one time or another. Do you resonate with the struggle conveyed in these words?

Meditation ::.

Bright days (in life) will not last forever, and sometimes you will be so devoid of all devout and Godly feelings that it will seem to you that your soul is a desert land, fruitless, sterile, wherein you can find no path leading to God, no drop of the waters of grace to soften the dryness which threatens to choke out your life entirely. It is very true that at such a time the soul is greatly to be pitied, above all, when this trouble presses heavily, for then, like David, his food are tears day and night, while the enemy strives to drive it to despair, crying out, "Where is your God? How do you think you will find him, or how will you ever find again the joy of His Holy Glory?"

— From *An Introduction to the Devout Life* by Saint Francis de Sales

How do you respond when you find yourself spiritually dry?

Read Mark 1 but focus on these verses: 9-13, 35-36.

Meditation ::.

"The great joy of the Saharan novitiate (a novice to the desert) is the solitude, and the joy of solitude—silence, true silence, which penetrates everywhere and invades one's whole being, speaking to the soul with wonderful new strength unknown to men to whom this silence means nothing."

— From *Letters From the Desert* by Carlo Carretto

Are you able to sit in silence? For many of us, silence and meditation seem nearly impossible, simply because we never experience them; we never put ourselves in a place of silence and stillness. There is always something going, an iPod, iPad, phone or computer. We are texting, tweeting or checking in to some social media portal at all hours of the day and night. Many of us have never imagined the joy of silence and solitude and have ordered our lives in a way that we are not capable of attaining it. I think this is often why we find ourselves in the desert, where we have no other option but to wait for the Lord. The desert forces us to be still.

How might you take advantage of your silent desert moments?

LENT :: Sunday #2

| Genesis 17:1-7, 15-16 | Romans 4:13-25 |
| Psalm 22:23-30 | Mark 8:31-38 |

TEMPT

"Because he himself suffered when he was tempted, he is able to help those who are being tempted."

Temptation is a very real part of any desert experience—but we are reminded even when it strikes at our very core that Jesus fully understands this desert battle. When it seems to grow stronger by the day, He has been there and is here with us.

Meditation ::.

"Three Gospels begin, after all, with an account of Jesus's temptation in the wilderness (Matthew 4:1-11 and parallels), and though these abbreviated and stylized accounts can be misread as an apparently rather easy victory, we are no doubt meant to understand that these were severe and prolonged attacks on the very heart of Jesus's understanding of his own vocation and identity and the character of the kingdom he was called to inaugurate. Successful resistance to temptation may result in an increase in moral muscle, but that's because one is going to need it; a temptation resisted may become more, not less, fierce, since to give in is to decrease the tension, at least for the moment."

— From *After You Believe: Why Christian Character Matters.*
by N.T. Wright

What is stirred in your heart and mind when you think about
Jesus being tempted just like you are?

Meditation ::.

"What is the gift of sorrow? It is so natural to want to come up with a positive side to sorrow. "God must have wanted me to learn [fill in the blank]." I think that the gift of sorrow is the same gift that we receive during Lent, Holy Week, and Easter. The gift of sorrow is God's loving and compassionate presence with us—in whatever we are experiencing. God in Christ walked through the human experience of suffering. And God cradles us in our tears, our hopelessness, our grief, and our sorrow."

— From *Alive Now*, March/April 2011 by Beth Richardson

It's true, isn't it? We often just want the way out, rather than the One who can give us comfort in the midst of suffering. I think this is precisely why the One who could give us the way out sometimes chooses not to. Instead, we receive the true gift of God Himself, not only what He can give us. My prayer is that during this time of Lent, we would seek God's face when we are tempted and tried, and not just His help to get out of temptation.

Our reading for today says, "God is faithful; he will not let you be tempted beyond what you can bear. But when you are tempted, he will also provide a way out so that you can endure it."

That is God's nature.
How often do you seek the gift rather than the Giver?

In the desert, temptation is inevitable. Even Jesus faced temptation in the desert, which is a large part of what we are thinking about this week. But often we forget that we are not alone, that Jesus is with us even in the midst of temptation, that He understands. Instead, we feel buried and full of despair. It's easy when temptation is at its zenith (and you've most likely given in at least once) to forget the grace and presence of God. But remember, the Spirit of the Lord is with you and in you.

Meditation ::.

"Have you ever watched a great burning furnace heaped up with ashes? Look at it some ten or twelve hours afterwards, and there will scarce be any living fire there, or only a little smoldering in the very heart of it. Nevertheless, if you can find that tiny lingering spark, it will suffice to rekindle the extinguished flames. So it is with love, which is the true spiritual life amid our greatest, most active temptation. Temptation, flinging its delight into the inferior parts of the soul, covers our soul entirely with ashes, and leaves but a little spark of God's Love, which can be found nowhere except far down in the heart and mind, and even that is hard to find. But nevertheless it is there, since however troubled we may have been in the body and mind, we firmly resolved not to consent to sin or the temptation thereto, and that delight of the exterior man was rejected by the interior spirit. Thus though our will may have been thoroughly beset by the temptation, it was not conquered, and so we are certain that all such delight was involuntary, and consequently not sinful."

— From *An Introduction to the Devout Life* by Saint Francis de Sales
(Language slightly modified for the modern reader)

How do our temptations reflect our most inner weakness?
What would change if we truly believed Jesus can meet us
in even the most barren and dry parts of our lives,
teaching us how to resist the devil and the temptations we face?

During Lent, it's helpful to use Christian icons as a powerful means of meditation. Icons are not meant to be accurate depictions of a historical event but rather an image, a piece of art that points to a spiritual reality that has taken place. Rowan Williams puts it like this: "(Icons) are—like our efforts in Christian living—human actions that seek to be open to God's action."
The Lent Web Guide contains two icons that depict temptation: that of Jesus and that of Adam and Eve. As we spend this week of prayer and self-examination specifically focusing on temptation, remember that only Christ has done it perfectly. Our journey with Him in the wilderness full of temptation is about learning to lean into Him, learn from Him and be filled with Him so that we might, through His grace, also have victory in the midst of temptation.

In addition to the icons on the Lent Web Guide, you'll find a link to Rowan Williams' book, *The Dwelling of the Light: Praying with Icons of Christ.* Make sure you check out this great devotional resource.

Where do you find hope in the midst of temptation? What objects or images can you use to help remind you to seek the hope we have in Jesus?

Consider this: The influencers in your life pull you in the direction they are going—and at an ever-increasing pace. That's because the more familiar you get with someone and the better your friendship is, the further and faster you're willing to go with that person. Oswald Chambers connects this relational reality to both character and temptation. God elevates character, drawing us upward into greater levels of Christ-like character in our own lives. The Evil One draws us into temptation that depletes the character of Christ in our lives. Who are you allowing to most influence your character?

Meditation ::.

"A higher state of mind and spiritual vision can only be achieved through the higher practice of personal character. If you live up to the highest and best that you know in the outer level of your life, God will continually say to you, "Friend, come even higher." There is also a continual rule in temptation which calls you to go higher; but when you do, you only encounter other temptations and character traits. Both God and Satan use the strategy of elevation, but Satan uses it in temptation, and the effect is quite different. When the devil elevates you to a certain place, he causes you to fasten your idea of what holiness is far beyond what flesh and blood could ever bear or achieve. Your life becomes a spiritual acrobatic performance high atop a steeple. You cling to it, trying to maintain your balance and daring you not to move. But when God elevates you by His grace into heavenly places, you find a vast plateau where you can move about with ease.

Your growth in grace is not measured by the fact that you haven't turned back, but that you have an insight and understanding into where you are spiritually. Have you heard God say, "Come up higher," not audibly on the outer level, but to the innermost part of your character?"

— *From My Utmost for His Highest* by Oswald Chambers

As you do the hard work of introspection, is the character of Christ increasing or decreasing in your life?

At times in the Christian life, it's hard to know what to pray. It is during these times that our spiritual community, past and present, gathers around us, and we find tools like a prayer book, hymnal and especially the Bible itself give us deep, beautiful and meaningful prayers to pray.

Often, it's in the midst of temptation that we lack the words. Here are a couple of prayers for you to pray during your desert journey.

"O Lord and Master of my life! Take from me the spirit of sloth, faint-heartedness, lust of power, and idle talk. But give rather the spirit of chastity, humility, patience, and love to Thy servant. Yea, O Lord and King! Grant me to see my own errors and not to judge my brother; For thou art blessed unto ages of ages. Amen."

───────────────

"Let us fast O faithful from corrupting snares, from harmful passions, So that we may acquire life from the divine cross and return with the good thief to our initial home."

— From *Great Lent: Journey to Pascha* by Alexander Schmemann

Let these two Lenten prayers ground you and guide you as you continue your journey.

We often see the ways others have given in to temptation,
but are we aware of our own temptations and failures?

LENT :: Sunday #3

Exodus 20:1-7 1 | Corinthians 1:18-25
Psalm 19 | John 2:13-22

AWARE

"Better is one day in your courts than a thousand elsewhere; I would rather be a doorkeeper in the house of my God than dwell in the tents of the wicked. For the LORD God is a sun and shield; the LORD bestows favor and honor; no good thing does he withhold from those whose walk is blameless."

There is always a temptation to think that in the desert God is absent. There is a temptation when we look inward to think that because of our junk, God will run away. This week we remember that despite our desert journey and the junk we carry, God is present.

The well-known monk Brother Lawrence wrote a spiritual classic entitled *Practice of the Presence of God*. It's one of those books that is timeless and relevant for every generation. During his simple duty of washing dishes, Brother Lawrence realized God was with him. He didn't have to be doing highly spiritual activities like praying, preaching or attending a church service. He realized that God's presence was always near.

I read this book a couple of years ago and this simple but profound truth has really stuck with me. I recommend you pick up the book at some point, but for now, go to the Lent Web Guide to read a few of his meaningful quotes.

Have you able to sense God's presence on this Lenten journey?

"Father God, Why is it that I think I must get somewhere, assume some position, be gathered together, or separated apart in the quiet of my study to pray?

Why is it that I feel that I have to go somewhere or do some particular act to find you, reach you, and talk with you?

Your presence is here.

In the city—on the busy bus, in the factory, in the cockpit of the airplane; in the hospital—in the patients' rooms, in the intensive care unit, in the waiting room; in the home—at dinner, in the bedroom, in the family room, at my workbench; in the car—in the parking lot, at the stoplight.

Lord, reveal your presence to me everywhere, and help me become aware of your presence each moment of the day. May your presence fill the non-answers, empty glances, and lonely times of my life. Amen."

— From *A Thirty-Day Experiment in Prayer by Robert Wood*
(taken from *A Guide to Prayer for Ministers and Other Servants*)

Are you as aware of God in the noise as you are in the stillness?
How can you become more aware of
His presence on the bus or at work or school?

It's really easy to breeze by this passage because it's a story that's familiar to us. And it's easy to get caught up in its supernatural oddness—after all, it's a burning bush. But when I stop and think for a minute, I realize that, yes, the bush is on fire and it's not burning up, but maybe the key to the entire story is that God is present. He inhabits the ordinary and His presence is found in the very things (an ordinary bush and some ordinary ground) that Moses has probably walked on and passed by the day before. The ground is holy just because God is present, and maybe if we were a little more aware, we would also notice His presence in the commonplace dirt and bushes of our lives.

Remember the promise in verse 12, "I will be with you..."

Meditation ::.

"A friend of mine says Christianity can be summed up in one word: awareness. On the spiritual path, mystics are those who are aware; their eyes have been opened to the things of God and they have "seen." They know themselves to be deeply loved by God, experiencing the Divine as the bedrock of all existence."

— *From Creativity and Divine Surprise* by Karla Kincannon

Experiment ::.

Go on a prayer walk. Center yourself in the love of God, and as you walk, photograph evidence of God's presence at work in the world with a digital camera. Go to the Lent Web Guide for more instruction and inspiration.

Where do you see God in the mundane,
the ordinary, the daily aspects of life?

I recommend reading all of Nehemiah Chapter 9, as it offers such a clear depiction of God's faithfulness and presence even in the desert. But focus on verse 21, a real snapshot of God's sustaining love.

It's interesting to me that Chapter 9 starts off with a scene reminiscent of Ash Wednesday. The ashes, pulling us back into this Lenten journey, help us not to forget where we started.

Contemplate God's desire to be near, to guide us as we wander around in the desert, as we fast and pray and seek His face. We can always know He is near, transforming us into His image and likeness—we just need to open our eyes and hearts and be aware!

Meditation ::.

"God does not hurry over things; time is his, not mine. And I, a little creature, a man, have been called to be transformed into God by sharing his life. And what transforms me is the charity (love) which he pours into my heart.

Love transforms me slowly into God.

But sin is still there, resisting this transformation, knowing how to, and actually saying 'no' to love.

Living in our selfishness means stopping at human limits and preventing our transformation into Divine Love. And until I am transformed, sharing the life of God, through love, I shall be (only) of 'this earth' and not of 'that heaven.'

And charity, or rather God's love, is what transforms us. What's the use of giving up everything and coming here to the desert and the heat, if only to resist love?"

— From *Letters From the Desert* by Carlo Carretto

Are you open to and aware of God's ever-present Love
to guide you and transform you, even in the desert?

It might seem like jumping ahead to Pentecost is a little out of place for Lent, but this week we are focusing on the idea that God through His Spirit is with us, even in our desert. Our ability to get to the Cross and our ability to say yes to the resurrected Jesus are gifts from the Spirit. We just need to open ourselves and be aware of Him!

Take time to slow down and feel the breeze, admire a sunset or just close your eyes and listen to His creation. Awareness is fostered by taking intentional moments to shrug off the hustle of daily life and embracing the pace we were created to live.

Make sure to check out the Lent Web Guide to look at a few powerful icons of Pentecost.

Remember: The Spirit is here—just open your eyes!

Do you live with your eyes open to the Spirit's presence in your life? How can you increase awareness of Him as you go about your daily tasks?

The key to spiritual vitality is simple: Be aware of God's constant presence in your life. But as simple as this sounds, we find it the hardest thing to embrace. The following meditation from Brother Lawrence is so profound because of this very truth. Awareness of God's presence is the "one thing necessary," but we must always work at it, becoming intentionally aware of this great gift that He is truly with us.

Meditation ::.

"God, says he, has infinite treasure to give, and we are satisfied with a little sensible devotion, which passes in a moment. Blind as we are, we hinder God and stop the current of His graces. But when He finds a soul filled with a lively faith, He pours into it his graces and favors plentifully. There they flow like a torrent that has found a passage, after being forcibly stopped against its ordinary course, and spreads itself with impetuosity and abundance.

Yes, we often stop this torrent by the little value we set upon it. But let us stop it no more. Let us enter into ourselves and break down the bank that hinders it. Let us make way for grace. Let us redeem the lost time, for perhaps we have but little left. Death follows us closely. Let us be well prepared for it, for we die but once and a miscarriage there is irretrievable. I say again, let us enter into ourselves. The time presses, there is no room for delay—our souls are at stake. I believe you have taken such effectual measures that you will not be surprised. I commend you for it—it is the one thing necessary. We must, nevertheless, always work at it, because not to advance in the spiritual life is to go back. But those who have the gale of the Holy Spirit go forward even in sleep. If the vessel of our soul is still tossed with winds and storms, let us awake the Lord, who reposes in it, and he will quickly calm the sea."

– From *Practice of the Presence of God* by Brother Lawrence

Are you advancing in your spiritual life or falling back?

| Numbers 21:4-9 | Ephesians 2:1-10 |
| Psalm 107:1-3, 17-22 | John 3:14-21 |

DESIRE

"All my longings lie open before you, Lord; my sighing is not hidden from you.

My heart pounds, my strength fails me; even the light has gone from my eyes."

It is in the desert of Lent, when you are saying "no" to surface level distractions, that your real desires begin to bubble to the surface. It is these desires for comfort, stability, acceptance, instant gratification and the like that our Lenten disciplines of fasting, self-denial and self-examination bring into light. These are the things deep in our lives that God wants to deal with. When we deny our desire for that latte or social media, we might have an initial craving for those things, but sooner than later, the underlying desire will bubble to the surface. What do we really crave?

These are the desires that we wish to give over to the Lord so that they don't control us like a bridle dominates a horse. If we let it, that is exactly how desire will function in our lives. Desire is about who we are just as much as what we have as we will learn throughout this week.

It's way too easy to try to bury or ignore our core desires. This is not the kind of self-denial we hope to embrace during Lent. Make sure as you look into and inspect the innermost corners of your heart and soul that you are honest and open to all that the Lord shows you. This type of honesty is the only way forward in full, abundant, resurrection kind of life.

> What are the longings, the desires that are bubbling
> to the surface for you during this Lenten journey?

Challenge: This week, share some of your desires with the community of folks you are journeying with.

Our culture idolizes getting what you want when you want it. But if we were honest, we would have to admit that if we instantly got everything we desired, things might not always work out in our favor. Often the best things that come our way are the things we have to wait for, or perhaps the things we never knew we wanted turn out to be better than anything we could have imagined. The following meditation helps us to think a bit deeper about the power of desire for the right things.

Meditation ::.

"Man follows his desire. One can even say man is desire, and this fundamental psychological truth about human nature is acknowledged by the Gospel: 'Where your treasure is,' says Christ, 'there shall your heart be.' A strong desire overcomes the natural limitations of man; when he passionately desires something he does things of which 'normally' he is incapable. The only question therefore, is whether we desire the right things, whether the power of desire in us is aimed at the right goal, or whether—in the words of the existentialist atheist, John Paul Sartre—man is a 'useless passion.'

Zacchaeus desired the 'right things;' he wanted to see and approach Christ.

Zacchaeus is 'short'—petty, sinful and limited—yet his desire overcomes all this. It 'forces' Christ's attention; it brings Christ to his home.

Ours is to desire that which is deepest and truest in ourselves, to acknowledge the thirst and hunger for the Absolute (God) which is in us whether we know it or not, and which, when we deviate from it and turn our desires away, makes us indeed a 'useless passion.' And if we desire deeply enough, strongly enough, Christ will respond."

— From *Great Lent: Journey to Pascha* by Alexander Schmemann

Do you desire Christ more than anything else?

"...and humanity became a living being."

I was flipping through my Twitter feed one day and read a C.S. Lewis quote that went something like this: "Man doesn't have a soul. Man has a body ... he is a soul." I affirm this truth and believe it to be true for all of humanity! In the Old Testament, a synonym for the word "soul" is desire. Let me explain.

The word translated "being" in Genesis 2 is central to our understanding of the Christian self. The Hebrew word (Hebrew is the original language of the Old Testament) is the word nepes. The word nepes can be translated a few different ways: Here it is translated "being," often it is translated "soul," and another common translation is "desire."

This Hebrew word is very nuanced and translators try to help us understand the intention and feel of the biblical writer by translating this same word in a handful of different ways. But the bottom line is that we don't just have a bunch of desires—we are one big desire; our being is a desire. You might read Genesis 2 like this:

"The Lord formed man from the dust of the ground and breathed into his nostrils the breath of life, and man became a living desire."

As exemplified in the story of Zacchaeus from yesterday's reading, the question becomes not if you have desire but what you desire. This is really the heart of the matter. May your desire be for Jesus, the living water!

What are you pursuing with your desire? What is your soul craving?

I'll be honest: I get distracted a lot of the time, and I can't just blame it on Attention Deficit Disorder. Mostly, it's the way I have ordered my life and the things to which I give my time and attention. The fact is there are so many things in life that distract us from the good gifts God has in store for us. Some of the distractions might even be good things. This meditation reminds us that with the help of the Holy Spirit, we must discern the desires that are good and from God and the desires that will only distract us from what is best.

Meditation ::.

Not every desire is of the Holy Spirit, even if it seems to a person right and good. It is difficult to judge truly whether a good spirit or an evil one drives you to desire this or that; or whether by your own spirit you are moved thereto. Many have been deceived in the end, who at first seemed to be led on by a good spirit. Therefore whatever occurs to the mind as desirable, must always be desired and prayed for in the fear of God, and with humility of heart; and most of all you must commit the whole matter to prayer, with special resignation of yourself, and you must say:

'O Lord, you know what is best for us, let this or that be done, as you will. Give what you will, and how much you will, and when you will. Deal with me as you think good, and as best pleases you, and is most for your honor. Set me where you will, and deal with me in all things just as you will. I am in your hands: turn me around and turn me back again, which way so ever you please. Behold, I am your servant, prepared for all things, for I desire not to live for myself, but for you; and oh that I could do it worthily and perfectly!'"

— From *The Imitation of Christ* by Thomas a Kempis
(Some language slightly modified for the modern reader.)

What desires sidetrack you and choke out the good that
God has stirred in your soul? What are the primary ways
you discern good desires from distracting ones?

"Don't let sin reign in your mortal body so that you obey its evil desires. Do not offer any part of yourself to sin as an instrument of wickedness, but rather offer yourselves to God."

Meditation ::.

"We have in us spirit, soul, and what we do with that soul is our spirituality. At a very basic level, long before anything explicitly religious need be mentioned, it is true to say that if we do things which keep us energized and integrated, on fire and yet glued together, we have a healthy spirituality. Conversely, if our yearning drives us into actions which harden our insides or cause us to fall apart and die, then we have an unhealthy spirituality. Spirituality is about what we do with that incurable desire, the madness that comes from the gods within us."

The theologian Ronald Rolheiser really hits the nail on the head in our meditation for today. Our spirituality, our Christian life, is largely about what we do with our incurable, insatiable desire. We can fill it with relationships, food, drugs, success, money or any number of other things, but until we drink the living water that is Jesus, we will keep wandering back to whichever well we think might have what we need. In the desert of Lent we have a unique opportunity, as these desires bubble to the surface, to remember that our Hope is in the Lord, that He is our portion, He is our living water. We also reflect on the things we typically let satisfy, if only for a moment, our desire that can truly only be satisfied by the Lord. So we fast and we pray, we turn to Lord realizing that He and His overflowing resurrection waters are not far away.

— From *The Holy Longing: The Search For a Christian Spirituality*
by Ronald Rolheiser

What things do you typically let satisfy your desires, instead of the Lord?

DESIRE // DAY 32
READING :: Psalm 130

"I wait for the Lord, my soul waits and in his word I hope. My soul waits for the Lord more than those who watch for the morning, more than those who watch for the morning."

Meditation ::.

"The truth we must learn through faith: to wait on God. And this attitude of mind is not easy. This 'waiting,' this 'not making plans,' this 'searching the heavens,' this 'being silent' is one of the most important things we have to learn."

— *From Letters From the Desert* by Carlo Carretto
(Read the rest of this quote on the Lent Web Guide.
You won't be disappointed.)

The idea in this meditation is that waiting is key to mastering and properly directing our desire.

There is a power that comes in waiting. Talking about love, the great philosopher Soren Kierkegåård said that the longer one waits, the more profound the experience of love will be. When it comes to our desire, our thirst, our cravings, I believe this is true. After all, you can't enjoy a cup of water any more than when you are parched, and a loaf of bread never tastes as good as the day after a fast. Waiting is key to desiring the right things. When we wait for the Lord, by the grace of God, we begin to master desire instead of letting desire master us. The desert, our Lenten pilgrimage of prayer and fasting, is all a practice in the art of waiting and the discipline of desire.

What are you waiting for?
How is your waiting shaping your desire?

LENT :: Sunday #5

| Jeremiah 31:31-34 | Hebrews 5:5-10 |
| Psalm 51:1-12 | John 12:20-33 |

CROSSED

The cross was not just an event in the life of Jesus. The cross was the way Jesus lived His life—His style if you will. The cross and the crucifixion was simply the culmination of the entire life and ministry of Jesus. You see, Jesus was constantly thinking of others before He thought of Himself; He was always looking out for the poor and needy before He was concerned about Himself and His reputation. Jesus was always laying His life down for the sake of others. Each act of self-giving and sacrifice was Jesus living a particular style of life, a "cross style" of life, as one of my friends and mentors Stephen Manley calls it.

In the midst of this life "style" Jesus was living, He stands up and says to his listeners, "Pick up your cross and carry it daily." At first, this seems like a peculiar invitation or command (depending on how you look at it), especially since this is pre-crucifixion for Jesus. But when you think about how Jesus has been and is living His life, it makes total sense.

Jesus was inviting His followers to live the same style of life He was living.

In the desert, we can choose to contemplate how we have lived; we can examine our hearts and motives; we can once again hear this invitation to die to ourselves and come alive through the Spirit. We can accept the invitation to let Jesus live His life through us, a crucified people, following a crucified God, showing the world how to live in crucified communities.

"Come, follow me," Jesus invites. "And take up your cross."
Are you living a "cross style" kind of life?

Our passage today invites us into a cycle of life: the cycle of the cross. This cycle of life and death is the idea that some things have to die in order for other things to live. We know this to be true deep in our bones—we witness it in our daily lives. We see it in nature when the trees wither into nothingness, only to come alive in the spring. We see it when we bury a dead flower bulb in the ground, only for it to spring to life in all its colorful glory. We experience this cycle when we sit down at the table to eat our meals every day. The plant that at one time was connected to a life source is now cut down and dead, only to be eaten to give life to a growing body. I won't go into detail about the juicy steak or burger we also sit down to enjoy, but trust me, in order for you to eat and live, something had to die. It's just the way it is.

"If you put to death the misdeeds of the body, you will live."

Roland Rolheiser, in his masterful book *A Holy Longing*, says this: "This cycle is not something that we must undergo just once, at the moment of our deaths, when we lose our earthly lives as we know them. It is rather something we must undergo daily, in every aspect of our lives. Christ spoke of many deaths, of daily deaths, and of many risings and various· Pentecosts. The paschal mystery [the mystery of dying to live] is the secret to life. Ultimately our happiness depends upon properly undergoing it."

So it is true.

Some things must die in order for other things to live.

What needs to die in your life so that you can come alive
in all the ways God intended?

"I resolved to know nothing except Jesus Christ and him crucified."

When we seek to know Jesus, like Paul in Corinthians we are seeking to know Christ crucified. And when we step into the life of this crucified Jesus, we not only embrace Jesus but we embrace the cross. This reality is important to remember as we walk through the desert toward the cross to ultimately participate in the resurrection.

Meditation ::.

"Knowing God—having an appropriately awe-filled yet intimate relationship, or partnership, with the creator, redeemer, and sovereign of the universe—is and was the life goal of a faithful Jew. It is no less so for Paul. Paul characterizes himself as zealous—both before and after his first experience of Jesus as Messiah—in his pursuit of the means to this knowledge of God and its corresponding life of obedience. The initial and ongoing encounter with Jesus, however, reformulated his understanding of who God is and how God is most fully experienced. That the Messiah, God's Son, was sent by God to be crucified, and then raised by God, meant that somehow God and the cross were inextricably interrelated. This connection led Paul to see not only Jesus, but also God the 'father of our Lord Jesus Christ,' as defined by the cross."

— From *Cruciformity: Paul's Narrative Spirituality of the Cross*
by Michael J. Gorman

To embrace Jesus as love is one thing, but do you embrace Jesus
as crucified, actively participating in His cross?

"For you died, and your life is now hidden with Christ in God. When Christ, who is your life, appears, then you also will appear with him in glory."

Meditation ::.

"Am I willing to reduce myself down to simply 'me'? Am I determined enough to strip myself of all that my friends think of me, and all that I think of myself? Am I willing and determined to hand over my simple naked self to God? Once I am, He will immediately sanctify me completely, and my life will be free from being determined and persistent toward anything except God." (1 Thessalonians 5:23-24).

— From *My Utmost For His Highest* by Oswald Chambers
(Check out the Lent Web Guide for more of this meditation
entitled "Sanctification").

I believe that sanctification is letting Christ not just be a part of your life but be your life.

Sometimes the process of becoming sanctified, or who you were created to be, takes some sculpting. I once heard someone reference the famous David statue and point out that at one time, it was just a huge piece of rock. The David we see now was always there, but Michelangelo had to do some sculpting to reveal its full potential. Often the sculpting work of the cross in our lives is a painful process, but picture Michelangelo skillfully wielding his chisel, giving shape to a formless chunk of marble. That's exactly what God is doing as He sanctifies us. He is slowly sculpting us into the people he created for us to be. We feel this most acutely during Lent.

Imagine the endless creative potential if each of us would embrace the cross and let God sculpt us into His image and likeness.

May you be filled with the grace and mercy of God so that His life can be lived through your body, because that is sanctification!

Oftentimes, living up to profound words like the ones in Bonhoeffer's meditation for today seem impossible. But it's during Lent that we ponder such important words and once again, pray that God would search us and know us, purify us and enable us to live into His call to carry our cross. Take a moment to realize that no matter how difficult this call may be, Jesus goes ahead of you and is with you. All you can do is hold tight and fast to Him.

Meditation ::.

"'If any want to become my followers, let them deny themselves.' Just as in denying Christ Peter said, 'I do not know the man,' so also should each disciple say this to herself or himself. Self-denial can never be defined as some profusion—be it ever so great—of individual acts of self- torment or of asceticism. It is not suicide, since there, too, a person's self-will can yet assert itself. Self-denial means knowing only Christ, and no longer oneself. It means seeing only Christ, who goes ahead of us, and no longer the path that is too difficult for us. Again, self-denial is saying only: He goes ahead of us; hold fast to him.

'...and take up their cross.' In his compassion, Jesus has prepared his disciples for this statement by speaking first of self-denial. Only if we have genuinely, completely forgotten ourselves, such that we no longer know ourselves, can we be prepared to bear the cross for his sake. If we know only him, then we no longer know the pain of our own cross, as we are seeing only him. If Jesus had not prepared us so amicably for this statement, we could not bear it. As it is, however, he has enabled us to perceive even this harsh statement as a blessing. We encounter it in the joy of discipleship, and draw strength from it."

—From *Meditations of the Cross* by Dietrich Bonhoeffer

How have you denied yourself and taken up your cross?

"Offer your entire lives as a living sacrifice, holy and pleasing to God."

Meditation ::.

"When this self-offering occurs, the results are nonconformity to this age—what Paul elsewhere calls 'death' or 'crucifixion' to the world—and transformation of the mind— what he elsewhere calls having the mind of Christ (Phil. 2:5; 1 Cor. 2:16), that is, conformity to Christ crucified. This transformation of the mind is the fruit only of a stance toward God that welcomes the divine power of the cross to effect change."

—From *Cruciformity: Paul's Narrative Spirituality of the Cross*
by Michael Gorman

When we embrace the cross of Christ, not only as theology or ideology but as a way of life, we embrace God's way of transformation. It is through sacrifice and self-giving love that all of creation will be made new; this is God's way. When we embrace the way of the cross—for example, by giving up a distracting habit or taking on a discipline as we do during our Lenten journey—it's something that we may not enjoy, but that we know to be a spiritually shaped sacrifice. We participate in this sacrificial transformation, not only of creation but also of our very lives. Living this way may help us to learn to truly live sacrificially throughout the rest of the year.

What is your reaction—positive or negative—to the idea of
living a cross-shaped sacrifice?

LENT :: Sunday #6
Palm Sunday

| Isaiah 50:4-9a | Philippians 2:5-11 |
| Psalm 31:9-16 | Mark 14:1 - 15:47 |

APPROACH

"When they approached Jerusalem..."

Jerusalem is the scene where it all goes down. This is the destination of our desert journey, the place where the winding road has been leading us. This is the place of the cross.

Yesterday was Palm Sunday, a confusing day where we remember the people of Jerusalem ushering Jesus into the city as a hero, then quickly turning to shouts of "Crucify Him! Crucify Him!" This is how we begin Holy Week. We have been looking forward to this deeply loaded and difficult week because as we approach the hardest time of the journey, we also approach its climax.

Jerusalem marks our imminent approach to the cross and ultimately to the resurrection.

I don't know about you, but a long desert journey, as this Lent has been, makes my bones ache for a resurrection.

Meditation ::.

"Holy Week can be a hard week. Jesus moves toward inevitable crucifixion. Those around him allow rage and cowardice to consume them. Friday brings sadness beyond measure...

Holy Week only works, however, if we put ourselves in the thick of it, which involves more than a grim determination to face the worst. It requires courage born of the knowledge that God's sovereign grace surrounds this week and our lives within this week."

— From *The Grace of a Hard but Holy Week* by Robbins Sims

Can you see yourself in that crowd? Where do you stand in the crowd that one minute shouts "Hosanna" and the next minute shouts "Crucify Him"?

"Holy Week, the seven days before the feast of Easter, from Palm Sunday morning to Holy Saturday night, is charged with meaning. It is a microcosm of Jesus' public life seen in bas-relief. All of its components are there—the population at large, the temple priests and their concern for orthodoxy, the prophetic words of Jesus and the political concerns of Roman officials for the social upheavals they feared could come from them, the arrest and isolations of Jesus, and the fears and confusion of His followers. Condensed into the one week, all these elements in the life of Jesus are laid bare for all to see. It is a dark week, a week heavy with the intensity of drama among them.

———————————————

We see all the forces of evil collude and collide. We watch as Jesus, caught in the grip of religious and political agendas, goes on speaking out doing good, regardless. No political spin here. Then, in the first part of the week—Monday, Tuesday, Wednesday—we get a glimpse into what will happen as a result. Jesus will die, yes, but not only. There is more than death to come."

— From *The Liturgical Year: The Spiraling Adventure of the Spiritual Life* by Joan Chittister

Experiment::.

I encourage you to try a little experiment with the story of Holy Week. Read it, sit in it, imagine the scene, put yourself in the sandals of a particular character and think about how the story feels from their perspective. Envision the hope, the despair. Do this a few different times from a few different perspectives. Really experience the emotions in the story. Visit our Lent Web Guide for some help with this experiment.

How would you have felt if you were in Jerusalem during Holy Week?

"Whenever we are following in the way of the cross, a moment will come when we say, 'If only there were some other way. If only God would stop the world, would make something happen so I didn't have to go through this process.' Jesus prays in Gethsemane that the cup might pass from him, yet he still affirms God's will rather than his own. He has come to the climax of all he has been doing up to this point. And so he prays (v.28), 'Father, glorify your name.' In other words: God my father, be God my father and be in and through me, so that the world may know and believe that you are God my father."

— From *Reflecting the Glory: Meditations for Living Christ's Life in the World* by N.T. Wright

During Lent, I frequently think, "I can't wait for Lent to be over!" I want to be done with the things I have added and I want back the things that I have subtracted. I just want to be done with this desert journey!

Who doesn't?

Whenever we find ourselves in the hard, dry places of life, it's normal to want out, to want things to change. Jesus did. But in the middle of His desire for things to be different and for an easier way to be provided, He prays, "I want you to be made known, Father, more than I want anything else." This is the example Jesus gives us.

As we approach the difficulty of our cross, will we want out or will we want God, His plan and purpose, His very self to be made known to us and through us? If we will follow Him to the cross, He will be lifted up in and through us, and He will be made known to us and through us.

Will you let the desert refine you so that God might be glorified?

"O my God, I cry in the daytime, but you do not answer,
by night as well, but I find no rest."

Tenebrae is a service of shadows that typically takes place during Holy Week. For the last few years during my Lenten journey, I have participated in this service at my local church. At the end, as we sit in silence, the lights are slowly extinguished, leading us into the days of Christ's passion. We are entering into the darkness of Jesus' death.

If you can, attend a Tenebrae service. It is helpful to hear Psalms and other scriptures that slowly usher us into the darkness and give us moments to ponder our Lenten journey as it nears its silent, dark and climactic conclusion in the death of Jesus when the skies turn black. Last year I participated in a more non-traditional version of this service of shadows. In addition to the traditional blowing out of the candles and reading of scripture, we watched videos containing imagery and lyrics that drew us into this darkening that takes place in the room and in our souls.

We embrace the shadows knowing that the light of the resurrection is right around the corner. Continue to remember that God wants to do important things in your life as you wander in the desert, in the darkness, searching for that which you have not yet found.

Visit the Lent Web Guide to view a video by U2. Let it draw you into the moment.

Do you feel the darkness of the shadows?
Are you still embracing the desert as you approach resurrection?

GOOD FRIDAY
READING :: Matthew 27:32-53

"My God, My God, why have you forsaken me?"

Complexity and mystery are at their peak in this moment where God is crucified, fully present and hanging on a tree, but at the same time absent, turning His face from the sin being assumed by Jesus. In the middle of Jesus' darkest moment—paradoxically when He was glorified or lifted the highest—He leans into the Psalms to express what He is feeling, namely Psalm 22.

In the middle of one of the hardest times in my life, when it seemed like my world was imploding and the people I called family had abandoned me, I too leaned into the Psalms and found one that lamented with me, that asked the questions I was asking and sought God in a way I was trying to seek Him.

The Psalm I read begs the question, "What are the right sacrifices?" Psalm 22, the Psalm Jesus had in mind, asks for mercy, deliverance and vindication as many of them do. The Psalmist asks God to lead as He had in the past, even though it seemed like He might not be anywhere to be found.

I leaned into these songs and prayers because they echoed what my soul felt, what I was longing for, and they resonated with my circumstances.

In the middle of Jesus' darkest moment, He leans into Psalm 22:

"My God, My God, why have you forsaken me?"
Why are you so far from helping me?

Jesus is asking God, with an honest gasp and familiar prayer from the scriptures, "Father God, where are you?"

Reread verses 50-53.
"And when Jesus had cried out again in a loud voice, he gave up his spirit. At that moment the curtain of the temple was torn in two from top to bottom. The earth shook and the rocks split. The tombs broke open and the bodies of many holy people who had died were raised to life."
Kind of wild, right?

It's a cosmic moment. All has gone dark, as if everything, if only for these few moments, has disappeared and in its reemergence, all of history has shifted. Something is different. There is a new nexus to all of human history.

Everything that happened before, we now know, wasn't just linear history but a string of moments leading up to this moment. Everything that will happen after this is situated in reference to this moment.

Human history no longer has a beginning and an end. It has a middle.

History has been reoriented and its new center is the cross of Christ.

And as dark as this moment is, we find ourselves wanting to call it good news and celebrate this dark day as Good Friday. We live in this tension and embrace it as mystery.

It's in this central moment in human history that we find Jesus leaning into the Psalms, wondering where the father has gone, revealing to us his humanity.

It's also in this central moment that we find our greatest fear and our greatest hope. Our greatest fear is that God has abandoned us, if He was ever there in the first place. Our greatest hope is that this isn't the end of the story for Jesus or for us—that in suffering there is hope, that this is really just a new beginning of sorts.

So where was God while Jesus was hanging on the cross?

Will Willimon says, "It's on the cross where we see the complexity of the way that this God saves us, the curious way in which God is with us."

God didn't save Jesus from the cross, but He schemed of a way to make this event one that nobody would ever forget. God schemed of a way to subvert the message of this horrific event of the cross, this political statement that was being made, and proclaim a different statement of hope and victory.

God is not like humans. He does things very differently than we would want him to do things.

Willimon also says, "We ask Jesus to stand up and act like God and he just hangs there."

God chooses not to use coercion but love, service and self- sacrifice, because they are His way.

Think about your greatest moment of darkness. Whether you realized it or not, God was scheming of a way to subvert the message of despair being proclaimed in your life and circumstances and to proclaim hope. He always schemes and dreams of ways to bring light out of our darkness, hope out of our despair, good news from all the bad news we find ourselves living.

On all the Fridays of our lives, when with Jesus we want to say, "God, where are you?" maybe He is just hanging there, present and absent all at the same time, waiting for the subversion of your story and ultimately His story to be proclaimed. After all, Sunday isn't far away.

What is your cross, your Good Friday?
Have you forgotten that Sunday is coming?

Holy / Black Saturday
READING :: MARK 15:33-47

John 19:30 records Jesus saying, "It is finished." And the Apostles Creed says that Jesus "was crucified, died, and was buried; he descended into hell."

Today is Holy Saturday or Black Saturday, and we meditate on these words of Jesus. We ponder the mystery of Jesus, the second member of the Trinity crucified, dead and buried.

Go to the Lent Web Guide to see a few images to help you as you sit in the darkness of this day.

EASTER SUNDAY

| Isaiah 25:6-9 | Acts 10:34-43 |
| Psalm 118:1-2, 14-24 | Mark 16:1-8 |

HE IS RISEN

.:: RESURRECTION :: Eastertide

Welcome to Eastertide!

Eastertide is the 50 days between Easter Sunday and Pentecost. It's a huge party! Every Sunday is considered Easter Sunday during this time.

I like the idea of Eastertide being a party because all too often the Christian life is perceived as serious and lacking fun and enjoyment. Our culture perceives Christians as "those people who can't do anything fun." How did they get that idea? We participate in resurrection! Yes, we might spend some time giving up something or adding on some extra disciplines to tend the garden of our soul, but we also should be known for possessing more joy and life than anyone else. After all, Jesus came to give us abundant life (John 10:10).

So let's prove it!

Use this next season in the life of the Church to walk in the joy of the Lord (Nehemiah 8:9-11). Show the world how to live the abundant life that Jesus offers to all who participate in resurrection!

Make sure you check out the Lent Web Guide to view a couple of videos that are sure to inspire you as you walk in the creative, joyful, abundant life of a resurrection people!

Go to love and serve the Lord
in the power of the resurrected Christ! Amen!

web : www.erikwillits.com
blog : ww.erikwillitsblog.com
email : erik@erikwillits.com
twitter : twitter.com/erikwillits
facebook : facebook.com/erikwillits
instagram : erikwillits